The Afterlife of Sweetness

THE JOURNAL CHARLES B. WHEELER POETRY PRIZE

The Afterlife of Sweetness

Poems

Jaia Hamid Bashir

MAD CREEK BOOKS, AN IMPRINT OF
THE OHIO STATE UNIVERSITY PRESS
COLUMBUS

Library of Congress Cataloging-in-Publication Data available online at https://catalog.loc.gov
LCCN: 2025043761

Cover design by adam bohannon
Text design by Stuart Rodriguez
Type set in Adobe Garamond Pro

♾ The paper used in this publication meets the minimum requirements of the American National Standard for Information Sciences—Permanence of Paper for Printed Library Materials. ANSI Z39.48-1992.

For Paradise

"Pollen der blühenden Gottheit."

—Rainer Maria Rilke, "Die Zwiete Elegy," from *Duineser Elegien*

Contents

III. FANAA OR UNPARADISE

I
Sacred Rot

Stringing the Bow

Driving in the American West, reading Celan
and the Mahabharata. After the war,
Arjuna drops his bow forged by Brahma back
into the ocean, part weapon,
part offering. Before drowning
in the Seine, Paul Celan wrote, *the beloved*
is an *arrowy one.* Brahmic time is cyclic
and malleable as the blue dress billowing
against an indigo wind. In this mining town,
echoes of an escaped two-headed
calf orbit an abandoned truck,
rusted metal and the living. *Christ!* someone said,
like a Hindu god! Yes, the many faces
of time and love's arrows veer
from each nock. *Where are you*
going now? Driving on the highway past
unmoved animals. Their boredom larger
than mortality. In my own boredom
I'm consumed by beloveds. The beloved:
a sharpness. The beloved
as an arc. *Time createth all things*
and Time destroyeth all creatures, this line
glowing in gas-station neon. In a parallel universe,
Celan, is drawn onto the bridge, shoes spilling water,
lungs pressed back into rhythm. Verse after verse, I've prayed
in round and rearview mirrors. Blessed with multiplying
faces and bewilderment, I take a turn
off the map. I underline Celan: *Reality is not*
simply there, it does not simply exist; it must be
sought out and won. Time opens its hand.
I am so afraid of ends.

Maggotville

Is this a way to live?
I lift the cover of the garbage bin.
There, a ghastly citadel. Numinous
maggots writhing in unfurl. Some
lives like these appear due to forgetfulness.
Pale flesh confetti. Where are their eyes?
Bodies like constellations stuck
on black plastic with no astrology
to offer. I don't feel disgust;
just shame that we, too, cannot
coexist. I close the lid and take
the bin to the curb, the weekly
garbage pile, to be eaten
by other scavengers, inducing a world
of new thoughts. A way of arriving
in the hot rot of fruit and pulp fever.
I tried to tell you over dinner—
Hey, can you imagine a world where
we were intelligent enough to build
from vestiges? To rely on a rotting
cosmology? To fruit something
from soft remains? Where we could
take waste and make it good? You didn't
listen. Blood from the uncooked venison dripped
down to the linoleum. And we went on and on
wordlessly with our frozen meal.

Marrow of Mercy

Releasing the half-eaten olive from my lips
I create a goat's eye in the center
of my white plate as the evening chews

an assemblage of darkness. I kite
my hands over flames as if I control
the underworld as a banquet

or pestilence. Eating is an obedience
to this one body. I only exist
secondhand. People's hands

have been through each sleeve
before me. In a Gabriel García Márquez
story, two lovers don't touch, only meet

in their dreams. Then, upon awakening, repeat
a solemn refrain: *ojos de perro azul.* Last night, I dreamt
of my old lovers. I don't have any friends.

I begged them to stay and repeat "eyes
of a blue goat" in Urdu. یلی بکری کی آنکھ.
Etched delicate, the animal's snowy belly

white as a slice of winter pear. The hoof,
god-cobbled black, stamped the ground.
It left tallies. It knew choreography.

Everything is more beautiful in Urdu
and Spanish. I have a book report:
I looked into their pupils, and no dog

I know is blue; they all seem happy.
My sky-eyed husky killed everything
that entered our dark field. We found

the black-gloved paws of squirrels.
Only thieves in the animal kingdom
have hands like ours. Raccoons, possums,

and ungodly monkeys who swarmed my halo-
blonde acquaintance touristing India. She messages:
I understand why you worship them. They are weird

like people. I'm Muslim. My old dog slept outside, but we loved
him more than ourselves. I only like dogs
and dogs in this life. When I walk down

the street, I hate making eye contact. Instead, I pray
to Allah for mercy for every earthworm.
Ultimately, I want to be eaten

with gentleness in my departure, as I was
nurtured upon arrival. When I was young, Ma
cooked mutton fresh. Despite its braying, I strung

a pretty ribbon bow, the evening before goat-Eid,
a token of tender despair around the animal's neck.

Good girl.

Good Girl

At first, harmless—an accidental lullaby stretched
across the headlights of an overnight truck
on an empty highway. Then, it alters. As a child,—

half alms, half alarm, I was called an *angel*. Yet, I remember
pressing my mouth to the lips of the sexy villain
on the old Panasonic, swallowing static. Then, later,

I rejected all my matches on Valentine's Day.
Engrossed by Venus at the Met. Her belly, a full moon
above a graveyard. Naked cupid dangled over

like an afterthought. Then the night arrived,
a song of the same old shadows. I've only craved
words of affirmation: *You are such a good girl.* So, tell me

to undress, as Titian's Venus, to wait
at the window—I'll wait for my lover who left
his wife, tuning his sorrow and Spanish guitar on the edge

of my messy bed. I am a hunger artist. To devour
is to destroy. I can't fast on holy days. This interior
false god feeds on meat, fat, sardines, black olives,

and all others forbidden and rotten. A parable
in Islam reveals a prostitute lowered her shoe into a well
for a thirsty dog. That one good deed and God's grace fell

around her in warm rain. I just want one drop of mercy
on a long stain. The rind is the rule, the reward is holding in
sweetness. I eat the entire orangerie: glass and flesh.

Now even dawn withdraws its touch. If only goodness were mine to claim.

The Strangers

I was standing in front of an old house
where an unremarkable schoolboy first took off
my bra and ran his hand over the band
of my underwear. He never found
the oldies station on the radio. I stuck
pink gum under his bed. Hot grass curled
in his cleats. Cold lemonade. The Venus
flytrap traded from the one-eyed butcher's
yard sale on the window. Nothing spelled out
from the seeds of inedible fruit smashed
on the sidewalk. He moved away
and has children now. I returned
to our hometown. I never wanted to.
Recently, a stranger confessed his GPS
speaks more kindly to him than his wife.
He then kissed me. I didn't return
a secret. I'll never see him again. Yesterday,
my dress unzipped at the sushi bar,
my back slick and pink from falling
asleep outside. My professor
cinched the silk together. I have no trouble eating
anything raw. The horseradish and imitation
fish went on pretending. Later, I took him
to my dirty, aging apartment. I live
alone—I'm letting out each dove
from a ruined cathedral. *I want you
to think I'm beautiful,* I said, my eyes closed
as he touched my body. Out by the meridian
of the street, an old woman appears. *Can I help
you?* There is no shelter in telling someone
about a life they didn't live. I get back
in my car. There are so many unfamiliar
freckles and acne marks in the afterlife.

The Waiters

Blued rags in my hands. We eat
the leftovers and shooed seconds of half mortals—
under each plate, quarter moons

hide before glow. In the empty parking lot
after bleached tables, we stand beside
and over rainbows, the outerglint on asphalt,

runoff from the gas station. Holding fires
to purple mouths—a strike of momentary beauty.
We smoke and gossip about the movements of stars.

With tired hands, generous still
to smooth currents—we are each other's

tangled black hair in nets. In the tight embrace
of no embers, no control over light.
Undoing my unlovely ponytail, caught dark

hair freed into directions of clocked-out air—
there are no borders here. In your palms, I am softening

our American name over callus in Nastaliq.

The Brute

Instead of the ocean, I pocket the moon
of an oyster shell from a dim restaurant
in Barcelona. We drink the dregs and boasts
of dead sailors, bitter and salt-heavy,
from the shell's mouth. The sea tastes sweeter
like this, and I forget about the gyres swirling
like black bulls, islands the size of cities. If I were plastic
I'd want to be shaped like a toy—gifted at the
zoo, left in the night mud of a child's forgotten field.
Sniffed at by wolves. Chewed up by cows.
She knows this, such a minor detail, my old crush,
the only person who's ever unpeeled me and left me
exposed before the flies could come. We play a game
of rhyming couplets. The clue: What does
a mermaid drink? *Sea tea!* one friend
shouts. *Brine wine!* says her
new lover. This dark, chic, noisy bar
is called Brutal, from brute, *belonging
to the animals.* An Ethiopian nun plays jazz
in the corner. My crush brings a cheetah-
print purse to the table. *For you,* she says,
in her dark purple voice. I bite the lemon
—whole—its burning light floods
my mouth, like Icarus caught on a rope
of sun. I open the gift: another cat, a small ocelot,
its mouth an open cave with jagged pearl teeth.
When I was young, crouched beneath the kitchen
table like a girl Mowgli, I smoothed my Ma's old fur
coat as an alternative pet. I wanted to animate
the inanimate. Everything possessed interiority.
For the mollusk, there is no life before the shell, but I
remember my world before touch, untouched,
places I thought would never be found.

On Hunger

Isn't that funny? An oyster has no mind,
just a mouth. Does it feel pleasure? my crush,
after meeting in Spain, latitudes and oceans apart, asks
from a historic apartment in Montmartre. The French call
oysters *fruits de mer.* What would it mean to be broken
into while living? The gravity of being
chiseled by a stone over a stone as if to make a sculpture.
Imbued in the light only the shipwrecked see. I, too, just want
to be a mouth. To just speak prayers of bewilderment. My masses
of nerves, no mind, tangled around this body
seeking, through pressure and pleasure, to create. A starter
mother is placed within an oyster and agitated to produce
a pearl. A nucleation. An inverse pregnancy. Forms
of divinity have also occurred this way.
I tell my crush, looking out the window at the cathedral,
talking about nuclear weapons: *The line in the Bhagavad Gita*
isn't "Now I am become Death." It is more like
"I am Time, the great destroyer of worlds." There is not
enough time on this phone call or any phone call. I've held
shells to my ear. Oceanic prophecy, each a folded fascicle.
I've eaten the center of a Rodin.
I sent this friend a letter. I was bereft
for weeks. Until their hands unfolded me
toward this nucleation. It said: *I want to be*
with you too. I meant that I wanted to be
the other mouth in all the meals we won't share,
and repeating this means there is an impossible
hunger wherever we are.

On Greek Origins

I was a winged child in the Indus
with the sun's preening of rain; I crafted
a private alphabet from the charcoal-
smeared darkness on my waterlines. Savored
gelled eggs cradled in ځ, a lone father
seahorse, and ate delicacies into ح.
My roti sank into the hum of dusk.
Intoxicated in the wine-fruit of ﺒ
I let fall the nuqtas, like pearls, one by one,
onto the eager mouths of minnows.
ⅡⅡⅡⅡⅡⅡ blades of grass—arched
into the fangs of an aleph. I clutched
ع onto a fleeting genesis. Everything was
in the throat of the world. Then, I started
to forget. The Maenads
night-bit Orpheus into pieces
for his lack of song. For in grieving,
the mouth is the first part
of the body to die. They threw his lips
into the maggoted soil. There, it opened
into م م م lips on a stem. I don't feel
descended from a lineage of bloodthirst
or greatness. I look down
into a year. Then, another. As if I could
cup its contents into the shape
my hands make in dua. I wore gold
Patagonia jackets. I went up the Rockies.
Then, I saw a dark I hadn't seen
before. Oh, God. I only want to know
you. How do I make animal calls
and realize it isn't an echo?

Self-Portrait of a Face That Isn't Mine

Each interaction—
the divorcee in a dim-lit bar, exchanging
coins with a cashier, the colleague who leaned in
after a meeting. Then, they all bore her face.
The curl of her hair, a script on rumpled sheets,
in the morning. She had cautioned,
while eating breakfast, *Don't keep a part of me.*
Get new things. A new life. Let go of us
when I leave. Yet, what of the claw
of a hairclip clung to the sprawling
mother of thousands? How her lips
moved while she dreamt. The stone and rust
she used to create pigments
from infested mud. The shining emerald
suspended between her collarbones
as she read a dog-eared Lorca, repeating:
Green, how I long for you, green. After her
departure, the man pried open a chrysalis
with the swiftness of unmasking royalty,
mistaking it for an exotic fruit. Inside,
only the unbirth of a monarch. A deceptive
womb. Who hasn't slipped into the heart
of lovers to take on a different geometry?
Finally, he extended his palms at the train
station, yearning to embrace strangers, to touch
everyone into recognition. This is how we endure:
pain must become a familiar. In the end, he pressed
his palms to his own face. Feeling the contours shift,
the loss of his Roman nose. The way his hair curled.
It was an alchemy akin to wings sprouting
on a creature unacquainted with flight.

The Cavesleepers

I can't stop tenderness. I want to mend
    the flattened red wingage of every lantern
        fly that lingers on a stranger's heels.
            Lapping water from my cupped palms,
    silken jowls brush against my skin. The mouth opens
and closes like a child's hand, signing for want.
        Your dog eyes have embraced being
nocturnal. The bereft summer,
        odors of wet earth and leather. I revere your phantom,
the lifelike yet lifeless flowers in the darkened yard—
        through photographs. We come to adore
the children we once were. Before you vanished
        and returned as a dog, how you sought to be Saturn
and devour yourself, all your children, and all your bones—
        the arrow with no arrival. The ball slung
again, and your impulse to follow. The canine-points
        of stars and extincted yellow.
Do you recall
    the cavesleepers who slept
for centuries? Their faithful dog's paws unfurled
    at the mouth of their time-dilated dreams?
In divinity school, this is how they explain time
    travel and the companionship of dogs in Islam,
In their centuries of rest, God did not abandon them or
rouse their dog. When they awoke,
        everyone had become
                a believer.

Then, the Cave

God sent spiders to web their filaments,
a net of mercy to save the beloved prophet
from his enemies as he hid
in a cave. Another story goes
time folded into itself—
a wrinkle, a trapdoor,
and a group of believers woke decades later,
their dog's paws pressed like relics
at the mouth of the stone quarry. The believers
found refuge in a stone mouth and awoke
into a different age. And so, spiders
are holy architects. I cup one in my palm,
a minor messenger with eight sermons
ready to scatter across the yard.
I watch its legs, mere wisps, stretch,
as if testing the patience of God.
Hours dissolve. I think of the spider
resting on my arm, its weight negligible, enough
to tilt the whole day. I hold the spider
on my abdomen, near my belly
button. That old mouth concave
with secrets, the sinful phantom I've taught
to swallow ash, to taste the burn
without complaint. A fire is a ravenous thing.
I know because inside of me is a burning
and I've fed it through my navel. Offered
my old name, my mirror, and endless hours.
I look down at my belly. The place
from which my Ma sustained me. I feed it
my woes and visions. My long hair. Once, I held
a spider to my belly button. Hoping it would web
over this first opening of myself. Then, I, too,
could shelter a believer inside.

Girlhood Rules Against Dating as Villanelle

What I couldn't. Sing underwater and desire,
on that surface dark alive, I learned to obey;
I sat in the soil halo of that cold. Fire

birthed in my body and breath, a choir
out of the spiral my navel. The Milky Way:
I couldn't sing underwater. And desire

turned us into adversaries. Ma, your higher
blooms sought to save, shadow me away
as I sat in the soil. Halo of that cold fire

where I am the mirror of you, that entire
girlhood of accepting stranger's tongues on Friday
and what I couldn't sing. Underwater, and desire

is budding into my pruned fingertips. I inspire
each boy's name I gurgle and love for the day;
I sat in. In the soil halo of that cold fire

you are my Ma, telling me to resist the pyre,
translating into me each name you can't say:
what I couldn't sing underwater and desire,
I sat in the soiled halo of that cold fire.

The Divine Dyslexia

Animal birth is nothing like you
imagine—the gross beauty isn't in the sudden

walking, slick-legged and unsteady. It's the hooves,
those God-cobbled shoes, folded tight

like prayers inside the belly, waiting—
the grassy smell of creatures, the bone anchor. The boy

on the farm and his slingshot, the sparrow's wing
snapped in two, *Dho,* and the quiet in the world

that keeps on going. Later, I help the farmer's wife
swaddle the lamb, its newborn shiver. It felt human

in my arms. Everything feels human
where we assign love. My Muslim Ma asked:
Why are animals in the nativity? Desire—

I miss you. *"Ek" means one,* but it echoes
like an *ache*—how it groans

from the inside; we aren't meant to do this
alone. What dissolves into the body, what lingers

at the back of the throat? A stranger once explained
how people see and misjudge the number line—placing a

thousand near the middle, between one
and a million. Numbers are terrifying, spilling over

what I can hold. I close my eyes and meditate
toward a thousand. The next day, I remember the lamb.

It died not so long after it was born.
It had no number line in this lifetime.

Found in the Congo, the Ishango bone is the oldest
evidence of arithmetic in our species—counting or

constellations. A geologist held up the animal bone,
studying the notches and evidence

of the mathematical mind. What were they accounting?
Spaces between births or the absence

between stars? I ask the spider to weave me a new veil.
I wear it to the mosque. A man blows the shofar

on the way, and a new year unwinds. I speak
a hundred names for God and one for myself.

Running my fingers on the mosque's smooth
emerald carpet to make tallies. Outside, folding inward—

the sky collapses into birds, into a murmuration.

Ek. Dho. Theen.

Ghost.

The Zikr Room

Once, in a dream, I drank water
from the vase tattooed on your shoulder.
Your name burned in my mouth.

I went to the Kusama exhibit in Los Angeles.
The Infinity Room. My father worked nearby
once as a weaver. I remembered him there.

Zikr is the act of remembering
by the recitation
and repetition of divine names.

I thought I might build you a room—
a public work
where I weave your name

from my father's yarn.
A loom fed by memory.
Punch cards, early code.

Each machine inherits the body—
its softness, its severing.

Electric sheep dream
about the grasses that we feed them.
Wool pulled from pink flesh,

then, the motherboard.

Your shoulder:
blade and bloom.
I've remembered *zikr.*

If you come,
I'll thread wool through your fingers
as you play jazz.

I'll write your name
in charcoal,
in ash,

in fire.

I'll speak it
until it is breath.
Until we vanish into an echo.

Visitors will enter the room.
They will kneel,
pray—

and we will not be there.

Girlish

In the thirsting hours, I became older,
and in this unwelcome, dust and draft,
the angel of lint, of yellowing wallpaper,
of Wellbutrin, the metal utensils making
their disjointed clamor. My Indian braid.
The sari I hang like a bedsheet. Out of step,
my grays curled like animals shooed in
a corner. Out of the fur of night's escape,
all this age won't make me a roving shadow;
my meadow mind in a lunatic and furious bloom.
Bare feet fault over floors wiped clear.
The halls are an esophagus tunnel, and each rich syllable
arrives inside the house. *I'm still a girl.* A syllable
more primal. It takes more of the mouth to say.
To be a girl is to be a fever. The last sign of a body
fighting itself. I am that pulp, that spit,
of a lip that grows dark fuzz if not dealt with.
My period-stained underwear hung
on the faucet, drooping like neglected houseplants.
The word itself is a curling and unrolling
of the tongue. Make of me that drunk vowel.
To be a girl or a woman is to be taught
to chew the plate only until hunger
remains.

In the Throats of Wild Things

St. Blaise, a Catholic saint, blesses the unwing
of the throat and all wild animals. The brute

tongue that resides in both, I've caught
in myself a wildness. The injured

frog cried, part eye, part skin
in its recognition. Asking to be healed,

I, too, am amphibian song, the dark field.
The regeneration of the heart in all

of its impossible unfoldings
without an ambit. My mind lives in these

twin skins returned, how slow
this wheel is. The kinetic fluid nest

of salamander eggs floating on a lone
cloud above the mountain, I cup

in the shape of prayer. A body
of water, once polluted. Reverted back

with the unruly sky into clarity
through mycological regeneration.

How will you heal me? *What Eden
can I rewind into like an old VHS tape?*

asks the widow; the spider ashed
in a shooed corner, the nirvana

of teeth among other teeth. The unloved
hounds at the ankles of the saint after

being trapped and poisoned. Let me pretend
I believe in something. A miracle:

the discovery of a species of birds
that makes garlands out of thorns.

A spider that would create a veil
for me to wear to the mosque. A two-headed

calf born with no bulls around for miles.
It is not enough for me to become

a believer. What will be enough?
The belly-up fish turned back

to abandoned bluegrass femur-long.
Of salamanders jellied in a pond.

How Kali is an ecologist,
saints, too, are ecologists in the way they always possessed

knowledge of both creation and destruction
as a type of ecstasy. How can I be good

in this life? In preparation for the hereafter?
No matter what prayer you purpose,

here are the cycles of remaking—
my patch of red and sour feral

strawberries, I planted summers ago. I place
them on my fingers like thumbtacks,

each a different size of my casual sins.

Lucky Rabbit's Foot

After all of this, I want to understand the arithmetic
of rabbits. Not multiplication, but the frenzy. I've cradled
the childhood shoe of a girl I once loved,

the leathery tongue weathered
through seasons. I've learned heartbreak,
without discipline, becomes as untallied

as rabbits in heat swelling in nightgrass.
The terror of numbers. I've grazed the globe
of a bunny's stomach, already promised

to rot. The eventual citadel of maggots.
I want to taste her nervous life's dark ringing
and electricity. The angora coat once waited

on the corner of my bed. The older man I knew
kissed my callused feet. Flecked with pink polish;
I once was a dancer. He said the curve

where I fractured my ankle was the most beautiful
part of my body. A rabbit's foot
hung on his keychain. Before putting on

his clothes, he held a finger to my lip: *Sweet bunny,
you are so good.* I ruin fences and consume fields.
An animal so tender, but meant to ravage.

As opaque as the final gaze of a dying dog.

II
Brine

In Dead Horse Point, We Are Alone

and you are telling me your new father
is being deported, as we ride past rivers

unrushed by summer. *Look.* This is how
our world has always been this fragile, how we are cut
from the navel and scattered. Desert water

evaporates before it wets Lahori lines
of orange trees. The fruit that taught us how to slice
our world. *Naranja* or *Naarangi* is a tart tautology.

Rhyming with nothing in America, a vibrating echo
in both Spanish and Hindi. *Naarangi*
traveled from India to Spain and was handed

in ravishing fists, like the Earth itself, by Marco Polo
to hungry monarchs. Crystallized and jeweled
arancini in Sicily. Carried in sweetened braids

of a small bride, or the dead-eyed unanimal
glint of guns. Transcribed as tangy *naranja*
into the New World. Silently,

j is left out there hanging
from its hook. It was half-night. Whispering
midnight is *aadhi-raat.* We leaned again

on the silver beams of a motorcycle sweetly christened
El Burro. Circling darkened eyes, tying
hammocks from scant trees, sewn out and in

air eddies of hummingbirds.
Covered in pine needles, we pointed,
singing names back in English. In Spanish.

In Hindi. *How can we say Father? Walls?*
Together? Escape? Sloughed skin
of rattlesnake breaks through

and under chains. The skin bleached
white in silverhurry of moon's or *chandini*'s
reflection. A spiral worn soft as the hand-

me-downs of our starving brown
grandmothers: *Abuela* and *Nani* across
latitudes who once ate orange

out of oranges, down to smiles
of slithering pulp and rind.
Rinsing my hands under the metallic tips

of common stars—
if we were to do it again, ride and die again
with you, *El Burro,* out there at half-night,

this time, ride and die again,
in the warm breath of our tent, I'd say
Salaam and hold you so

with the American choreography
of a pigskin flying
to be caught

by a child whose real father,
like yours, rode and died
and only returned

once.

The Eyeball Halves

1. FIRST EYE

Before incineration, my Father's eyeball
is placed into a plastic bag like a carnival

goldfish or lamb delved into butcher's
portions. As a child, I saw the head

of an animal my Father slaughtered
displayed on ice. Once ununited,

The head is never the body again. Memories
of how a *zamindar*'s mute

child was gifted multiple tongues:
arranged and alight on a woven bed

of white silk. From each came the dark
whimper of something's last

electricity before death. A severed ear
in Lahori dust remembers the morning

call to prayer played on the radio. How much
is about the displaced heart? Nothing

speaks without a body. My Father's retina
frayed, devastating for a weaver—his remaining

eye without a partner. I want someone
to know their litanies of vision.

2. SECOND EYE

This morning, hunger set me going
to write about reciprocation. An exchange
of eyeballs with a lover. Do you see

me now? It's summer again.
a humble swelter. Everyone is listening
to Kate Bush. Her voice through the static:

I'd get him to swap our places.

As though divinity might
allow the body to be
reconfigured.

but, if you took my eyes,
I'd ask you to recite Plath first:
I lift my eyes, and all is born again.

What would we resurrect?
Lovers say, *Give me your hands.*
Give me your heart. It isn't real.

But what if I said,
Give me your eyeballs
And meant it so tenderly.

I'd rinse them like grapes,
careful under the dripping faucet,
place them on a paper towel.

Once, I sat for hours
in the Hungarian Pastry Shop.
No appetite.

I tried to write something
as solid and sensual as Neruda.
I came up with: *Meet me tonight under your eyelids.*

Once, in his apartment, my professor
unzipped my dress, the sound like a blade,
slow and final,

he said, *I love your mind.*

I turned,
I said,
I just like your blue eyes.

They remind me of dogs.
They have a whimper to them.

There is an undeniable need there.

Con la Serpiente I

Tu boca manchada de granada. How many seeds
did you eat this winter? Dragging the fur of burrs
from the Underworld into these
> New York streets and parks. How many dogs
> did you see with three heads? To evade the laughter
> of a stranger's eyes. Abril, *Lejana y sola.*

Conoceme esta noche según tus manos. I'm your nailbeds
filled with flakes of my life before sleep. In April,
an electric unplugged eel is a liquid parenthesis.
> Speaking in octaves, searching for variations
> of hunger to speak to myself
> about your pomegranate-stained lips.

Mi lengua es esta serpiente   Mi lengua es esta serpiente   Mi lengua es esta serpiente

> In the Utah desert, on our knees, we witness
> serpents in wildflowers, mushroom circles
> like shoaling whales pooling around schools of fish.
Abril, *Lejana y sola.*
> Te seguiría a un inframundo

All things are cyclic. The swivel of an animal
that hears danger, Earth keeps returning
to the same position as our birthdays.

> I am in Harlem, again—
> someone has taken your mattress
> from the curb. You circumnavigate
the way blood journeys
through my body too. Moving on
in cyclic migration,
> or is it an instinctual movement?

Aleph from What Was Once a Homeland

EK / ایک

Ma Jaan holds ح from the end
of the clean-cotton of our *kurtas,*
British-English scented still

by Lahore. What is in its belly?
One pomegranate seed: ح
Three pomegranate seeds: ﭺ

Ma places an old gold pin in her mouth,
unmedaling her hair. Cutting the dead
-ends of braids ل in our front yard

to discard with the only working scissors
in the house. Lithe limbs of Kali
sprout another. Amphibians mimic

the goddess of death. Sieving through
my hair with yellow combs, searching
for roots that have become tinder,

others want to be on fire. Ma Jaan buries
hair into the underworld by the perennials. We go
to the *nikah* of two Pakistani strangers.

DHO / دو

At night, in the rain, over my shalwar-kameez,
a slunk, thrifted angora coat, the thickness
of my Father's knuckle hair. Blooming

from the mountains of his fists. Once,
I found a stray black rabbit. Its dead
language transmitted in the swivel-scissor ears

33

of its fear. After an evening of hiding in
ꟼꟼꟼꟼꟼꟼꟼꟼꟼ the moonshine that became mud. Then,
tracks of suburban mutts; I was once quick

to wash turmeric gilding the underline
of my nailbeds. د became a cuticle, a little
ر rabbit's foot touched infrequently.

THEEN / تین

Kufli glistens onto the tile after the colorless
sheen of another empty venue. Spilled biryani
forgotten. Here come the crows again, here

the pigeons, emerald-green of the Pakistani
flag that leans tired in my parent's garage.
The snout-cold of the neighbor's dog: ه

CHAR / چار

She always greets hello. The neighbor does not.
Once warm with bunny's blood, the grit
of her tongue. How many pomegranate kernels

are in my belly? Hymning on like Persephone
beneath the dayblaze, underworld combing her
hairline. What strata of the fossil record

are the jeweled rind and seeds mistaken
for small teeth? A lacuna, a spring,
grows after loss. How lavish the garbage

before the hawk-light, before the piledriver
will pick up our gross bouquets of marigolds
on a Tuesday. Again, the rabbits. ر

One Red Thread

Caminante, a pomegranate knows itself
    as numerous. There is a world, and it is here—
        inside this one. Woven with a naked light,
my Voyager I. *A tú manera si no con bandera.*
    Oh, and my *Caminante,*
        Voyager I journeyed
further than anyone, or anything, before. Did it look back
    over its shoulder, the same gaze
        of your blued departure to the borderlands?
Este retrato de Júpiter eres tú. Through hands
    and bread, we eat *Nihari* (نهاري).
        Arabic for morning, an aubade
of the body. Turning on the flames,
    pozole was once cooked
        from human flesh. *We believe
people are a type of maize,*
    lining hominy into a vertebrate.
        I'd devour your simple hunger,
El mundo es mundo. Your lips
    are two cochineal beetles or clouds pushed
        together to create such wrinkled time.
    I'd take *granata* always
        over a grenade. I've held each of your hands.
Caminante, our souls bristle in a field. Combed
    with the magnetic fields of stars. Our someday
        making *roti* and *tostada*
            as round as a horse's eye.

Brief Conversations with a Little Moon

Even this planet bears secrets, Little Moon.
Little Moon, you are an unfaithful lover roped in
    without siphoning the morning sky for clues.

A lover's hair that accidentally spells out love in cursive
    pulled into orbit with our vision concomitant
on both your glittering leaving and faint arrival.

There is no such thing as shared time in space,
    just private choreographies. We are often late
to the dance: two years of you, چاندنی and no light

    of knowledge, just cosmic squatting in an unseen circuit
above us without discovery. Gravity, a quiet thief, pockets
    small, cold unforever coins of the Universe.

Claims bodies with a bright sickle
    of wonder. Reaping in glitterfreeze,
sintering a handful of orbits, and then releasing.
    What will you tell the rest, Little Moon?

About what you witnessed on Earth?
    When will you return? Could we just be
another dim stone on the cairn of your travels?

    Little Moon, scuttled between planets
you are invisible to the naked eye that opens
    her mouth in warm zeroes. Then you will go

back into the dark ravine of an infinity

    that goes on without our favors, without our desires.

How to Make an Ariel

I've taken your shoes. Our feet
    are the same size, nothing else. Naked
foot where I touch an estuary

    of tubule-tender lines. Rambling into
a tarpan, heart beating with the warm rave
    of being a winning racehorse. Legs in a gait,

    I'm an unfaithful alphabet. Unwrung
English papers in the laundry room are slack
    warm sails that smell of the sea.

The humidity of my foreign palms. I am the hoof
    of us, recording every pain of every stone
that trots on the nail. The way we canter on it.

How muted my tantrum when you pointed
    to the unclean gravestone of my other grandmother.
Unknowable hypsometry of raised and curved

letters that I ran my hands over repeatedly.
    What does it say? A rolling wave of unknowing.
Do you love me, master? All my dreams are in English.

    Back at my Ma's childhood home.
I banded light. The generator deafening.
    Reading Shakespeare and practicing Urdu

in the bathtub, call me *Chandini,* moonlight. چاندنی
    Only so long before a lost American
mermaid can stand without floating on into foam.

    Where are we from sea level? How close to the lost
psalm written by walks intertwined—arm and fin.
    The rhythm made by feet clopping in

your bathroom slippers? In the wilds of myself,
    I *consider* you everywhere. In lines
of Paiute sandstone and burning sagebrush, I know

considerare shares an etymological root with *sidus,* or star.
    You have held me in the gaze of the most patient eye.

Shadows like lunar mares on the moon.

Brine

1. *EK* / ١١

Cold, telluric. The lake inhales
us whole: tin, salt, brine—

our bodies cleaving to the ache

of the Great Salt. Pink throat
and shore of the black-crowned
night heron. Hymning in the hot

white-hush. The mouth
of the lake. Salt-crust moons. When I was
young, I rode to the water's edge

with strangers who resembled
my father, where he pointed at the white distance.

This is where she's from, he says—
but I can't hear him. The night heron swallows
an entire desert inside himself.

Sagebrush. Buffalo bones. Hot, vacant sun.

2. *DHO* / ٢

Shores: mythologically whaleless,
bone-bright, dying—
a tang of the dead rising off its surface.

The land's memory is now a list of names:
Ute, Paiute, Shoshone—

Utes and Paiutes believe in water
babies, their cries reach you
if you listen long enough—if you're ready

to learn to swim. A baby is crying underwater.

A father teaching his daughter
how to say *water* in Urdu. آب.

Composed of two letters, alif (a) and bey (b).
This is where language starts. The aleph ‖‖‖‖‖

like the marshes of nightgrass, the bey
a ceramic used to wash our bodies and tongues ب ب ب ب

Bey as basin for tongue, *bey* for brine,
malleable as a newborn's skull, the arc
of what's too bitter to be swallowed whole.

3. *THEEN /* ۳

To brine is to preserve.

Father, I translate what the salt says.
You are (. . .)—and then it returns (. . .)

The brine, powdered, and pressed sea monkeys
will feed the king prawns of Asia. Guests

at a wedding will remark: *How odd—*

thumb and pointer squeezing the small body.

We contain landscapes. We eat them.

We disappear.

4. *CHAR /* ۴

Salt will pull the body up, hold you, *hold you—*
but the lake itself is drying up. Soon,

where I was born, the namesake
will turn to ash. Uninhabitable.

In Punjabi, the *dirt and dust and earth
you are made from is what you become.*

You can't drown in such saline waters.

Everything here holds its place: God into gravel,
snakes into asphalt, daughters—distant, burning.

We weigh the lake in our sleep.
We wake, still heavy, every morning.

From dust to dustbloom?

5. PANCH / ۵

Tonight, I turn the wheel along I-80
and imagine the lake beneath me.

The word *Punjab* comes from panch and ab:
the five waters. But I am from one body of water—
Great Salt Lake, brined, barbed, barren. The ب ب ب ب

hold nothing. July, the holy night rotting. Each wave

a rank prayer. *Question to self:* How many waters make a home?

Once, my friend said her daughter cries
nightly for her own body. To hold
herself again, small and contained.

She hands her a doll, lifelike.
But the child refuses.

We all know there is no return.
The Great Salt Lake dries,
I've learned to repeat: *ecological collapse.*

No baptism here—
one life pressed through the sieve

of the same bones,
brittle, porous. Not salvation, a thirst carried
from the mouth of one world to the next.

We're still so thirsty.

The past recedes
like salt retreating from tide. I hold

the lake in بـ. What can I carry?

Take it, I'll say—
first cry unlearned,
consonant soaked in silt, alphabet unborn—

Toward Tenderness, a Knife

Nani couldn't keep on living
without knowing the great voice of death.
    In her hands,
her last bird, cooing—*Ajo.* آو آو آو آو
Come on, in Urdu. The body
    rises for a moment. A boat bouncing
on trembles of waves. Spreading her hands
like a blind ascetic
    gathering paradise.
Circumnavigating fingers
on fat, ligneous neck, grazing—
    a fishing line
along the water, latitudes of home.
Comforting the chicken
    with palms that envelop mine.
Folding together
the dough, secret as fascicles
    to hide in drawers under saris,
bleached vermillion. The false breast
I once discovered, mistaking it
    for actual flesh
that Nani rushed to hide again.
Hear the whip
    of her three-pronged braid, swaying—
grown after chemo, a war medallion.
Breaching the neck
    with her favorite knife.
Calm as separating
meat from the pit of a peach.
    She hands me the heart.
A Ma who grew my Ma inside—
an immigrant to both worlds,
    could end a life, just as tenderly.
Later, I ask my Nani to send me her hair
from overseas. A gilt thread to weave
    on the throat
of my wrist, the same
length as my own,
    to dare the stained shadow of death—*Ajo.* آو آو آو

And the Word for Moonlight Is My Name

Hello.

Chandini. چاندنی

This mouth is a wound
    from which I'm learning how
to love. *My love language,* I've told strangers, *is words*
      of affirmation. In naked brag
        of my American tongue—how does it taste

      to love with this Indian
    body? I knew love being breastfed
through a nightstorm after the blue song
      of electricity ended. I parse each numerical line

    about starshine that arrives in tallies. *Chandini,* I've been
      the type of Western-methods
        coward who never listens

to my stomach's knowledge. I've taken
feverous temperatures with my hands.
    Then, gently slapped the trust
      of the thermometer on my knee
        and into a baby's mouth

    again. My nails are embedded with rinds of sweet oranges—
      always seeking the reach of knives.

Tell me the way
    the Bengal smells, a sweet perfume
nonexistent in a glass on my bedside table.
    Tell me again the way we could have known

how half gods carrying pipes with cloven hoofs
    sang in key to the slunk ring of rickshaws—
      the exhaust settled in laundry lines like blackbirds.

How to say my own name with the certainty of a dove
trusting the buoying ark of humanity. My bird ring
    patient and sliding on the tattoo of a birdcage.

Tell me again, *Chandini.*
        How divinity was without border control
            and conversing with the sky was as common as rain.

Ma used to preserve each of her calling cards in a glass
    vase as if they could blossom, as if they were the umbilical
rope tethering cosmonauts to the space station.

    Given the electric lines of your uncut braid,
        like an old telephone line operator,
            where can I connect it to, other than just myself?
Hello.

Chandini. چاندنی

I've held your hair with the softness of space saints
washing each other bare
    in zero gravity. Long-distance,
        on the other side, I'll be there,

    a voyager grounded after cosmic exile.
        My breath was on the line,
            just praying against echoes.

Hello.

                    Chandini. چاندنی

        Salaam.

45

Con la Serpiente II

Sleeping in craggy eights, deforming
socks and bedsheets. The fever
of the heat lamp watches the cat-eye
yellow of its prowl. Every escape
is an art form. God created
the serpent from mercury,
the glassy mirror in the basement.
To not frighten the mindless
and tender creatures loping
in the field. The night opens
a faucet of metallic light, the usual
chores. There, an ambush of stars
in a new dark. Now, each peel
of our skin in the kitchen
slinks on like gnarled bouquets
over a burial place. Between us—
sometimes that genre of silence.
We wash and eat bruised
strawberries swallowed whole.
Pink as tongues. Small as eyes.
It frightens me how much we can love
when starving. Where is the cage
now? Make of us
little beasts.

Still, Life with Fruit

Aanjir: Figs mirror bats.   A dark knowledge—
hanging in lines,   feral, swinging fruits.
Feline-faced anti-angels
drape from the roof.   Hugged in wings.   انجیر

Anar: *Granata!* If only the pin were just the thick star of a pomegranate.   انار

    Gajar: Biting down a blade to coin the body. *Halwa* chewed
    on a hungry Eid with *falooda*-stained teeth. Nani says to eat more
    for healthier eyes—whose visions are these?   گاجر

    Kela: The word for banana in Hindi is in proximity to the word
    for loneliness. I've shared twinned
    a-kela-ness with many—unfolding
    the stringy veils of our richness.   کیلا

Mooli: In Manhattan, carrying a bouquet of radishes. Earth buds:
spiced white and tectonic pink. Roots waltzed with loam,
sunlight appeared as a ligature. Hemmed letters of glow.   مولی

Nashpati: Sweet halves
in the shapes of ears part
to respond to dormant sweetness.

Holding two spring bodies
in my hands: A *pair* is not *pear*;
the rules of three in a still life.   ناشپاتی

    Saape: The American alphabet starts with an apple. After *salaat*, Ma
begins
cutting fruit. Skin spirals into rosettes from desert reptiles.   سیب

    Your Name: Before death, you are granted paradise if you speak
the *Shahada.* What if your name is my *Shahada*? Hawks take back the air—
and foxes fill fevered throats with mother's milk. Ma says *drink
this* in Urdu. I understand. Keep this secret.   شب بخی

Pegasus Tattoo on the Left

A horse is a muscular hyphen—
that connects humans to nighttides of the open
    animal world beyond us. Last night I dreamt
    that you married someone who wasn't me.
A winged horse is a regatta of stars—
human's first spacecraft, the moon, too,
    is a changing hoof. How far upward
    each verve of the earth, a lunarship searching
for unknown fruit. The tail, a brush of a comet's
glitterfreeze. I've sailed on these half wings.
    The dream rivets to silent, deep space.
    The event horizon: an open gate.
The cold ocean is not a horse—
Mare and *mer* false cognates.
    Lunar mare: dark waves
    of basalt, ancient stargazers misunderstood
to be water, *maria*. Pronounce this *Medusa*.
Sidus signs of your tongue on the lateral
    of my dark thighs. An odious oasis, a desert
    mer. Snakeskin glints in impastos of sage:
layers of landscape. I'll take handfuls
home with your old jackknife. I'll siren into
    chalk-smoke motes, shadowed patterns
    on celestial bodies. The mane falls wild
on my black coat. White heat from the planets
cantered light from behind the plateau.
    How far of a dive into *la mer* until each creature
    becomes eyeless?   Come, now, out of the sing of river—
drink a godsong like horses out of green
buds about to speak into spring.

¡Viviendo Así!

On a mountain

पहाड़ पर

sueño de ti.   *[dreaming of you]*   no harm

crossed over
no claims toward your sea

On a mountain

पहाड़ पर

no heartbreakers   मेरे दलि का सूरज
knew this world's heart.

por fin te vi

[I see you at last]

III

Fanaa or Unparadise

The Shadow Self

Against the naked wall, the ligatures of my fingers.
Scissors. Rabbit. Wolf. Then: God. Say *God.*
Thumper tells Bambi the names of things. I prayed

to God in the second grade for something
I could name. Shadow puppets cast against the rippled belly
of wallpaper. I wanted a diet of apples and figs.

Things that remember
what they were before
they fell. In my yard, there was a blackberry

bush—a thorn castle. T-shirts twisted into baskets. Mouths
spitting the bramble, preaching a fever. Tongue
gnarled. Mispronouncing salvation. Bambi trying to speak,

Bird! Bird! Then, I found all the speckled blood
down to the foundation of the house. After childhood,
I wear Margiela tabi boots and socks for hooves. Male deer die

of starvation after their antlers interlock. I learn of new violence.
Language is both a cage and a portal. I learn new
tactics and throw new shadows against the wall. Say *shadow*

at the one-eyed butcher's stall, where I request a new heart,
flesh, sinew, an ear, and a photograph of the butcher's bride.
I share these body parts with my lover—

twin aortas. Boiled the lungs.
Clinked glasses. Called it prayer.
I spread my hands out. They look like the fungi

populating quickly beneath the floorboards. *Please elevate*
the equator of this house. Give us altitude.

We remember paradise but can't remember
where it was misplaced.

Vultures, Then

I'm this obedient. The lammergeier batters
the lateral of a lamb's femur. Then, the vulture
drops bodies from the heavens. If Jesus, as a carpenter,

crafted the frame for a bed, I'd wish to dream there
indefinitely. A historian corrects me that Jesus
was a mason. His tools, hewn from shale and bone,

constructed houses for the people who would break
apart their rooms to cast stones
at their idle animals. Saints for the minutiae,

demons for the rest. In Islamic mythology,
there is a woman, part dog, part goat, devouring
men, genitalia and all, near the Red Sea.

Then, there is another creature: jewel-eyed
like a housefly's wings in paradise, caught
in the shape of a girl. Bestowed in the afterlife

upon faithful men for what else? Pleasures
beyond belief. I've taken wing
at the smallest disturbance. After midnight,

I was dreamless; my beloved held my waist
in three yawnfuls of darkness. What beast
am I? A peregrine force. As insubstantial,

as untethered as smoke. I've been
a girl with talons, and I've been that
domestic animal. To be elevated, then plummeted,

from an altitude where others locate
divinity. I know how to
fragment: each nail, the feathered hammer.

The Last of Us in the Wild

Teach each sawtooth, the dark mule
    of new words. Spare each dumb eyeball, reorder the optics
        from just new pollens. Weed us from ugly grasslands—

to unbetter bureaus. Bend over backward so often, to raise
    a new vertebrate, a new white piece to choreograph. To memorize: checkmate
        roped in from the gullies of Arabic, *shah mat,*

the king is dead. What they did to capture us, so lush
    and partially insane. To ask: *Can we fix the old paper of their soul?* Stained
        with coffee, warmed through each of our parent's fax machines—

breathing useless information, barely audible in a spider-whisper—
    a silence that makes you acutely aware
        of your own riversystem. From the benthic

    slathering off gills to shape into feet, to perform alchemy—
        the acrid, so gorgeous taste of our own psalm.
           To show us binary code. To ask: *How did we ever get so soft*

like twin lungs? How are you so strange?
        As if in gravity and buoyancy, the river song
           of ocean, there are not
        grotesque fish with bulbous heads, glowing
             to make their own light—
and when I move your gross scales mutely glinted too.
    All night the needle; all summer the sword—

    still, they can't just figure it out,

    as if examining a different species.

The Mouths

A bay, whaleless and surfless—and nothing lives
in water this polluted. Yet, someone insists

on having netted sardines here. We peel and savor
everything others say is delicious. *Bon Appétit*

sent a complimentary subscription. I searched
for the proper placement of accents. I'm afraid of mispronouncing

charcuterie and *oeuvre.* If I cease to create my body, no one will
recall these poems. *You could have*

gone to culinary school. I eat dollar ramen
when I watch *The Bear.* Plates scraped clean, I avoid

writing in favor of cooking. Relentless
sauces I spent years crafting cling to the corner

of a jam jar rinsed in a midnight siphon.
What did I keep fed and alive? A prayer

mat angled toward nowhere
we have visited. Hunger is a mechanical angel,

a dull annunciation of what will soon be
in the belly. My lover always asks about semiotics.

Not in a pretentious way. He wants to know
signs, like prophecies. Omens of writer's block

where I won't be happy. I want to name my child
after a character who is not always happy. Everything is

a sign if you look closely. I wrinkle as I age—the fauna
inside ferments. I craft wine. I scrape the gleaming armor

of salmon and lay it on stone to dry. I've borne these
scales and created more fish. The garland of garlic knocks

against the green door and the guests step
on wintery skins. I want to feed you. I want to make

you more dinner.

The Appalachian Trail

Where the old wind lives. The road is lunar, so it changes
            into a cuticle, black as dapples of aspen eyes.
Where you washed clothing and sat with the gasping perfume
        of catching fire. Where you walked through the lie
of only this life into another and then another. Where you wrote
                postcards unsent while watching slivers from the dark door of
another marked day. As if the Appalachian
was whistling back
            your soul in spite of constant evictions under the cool bark
            of the Dog Star scraping her claws.
    Will you always be a ranger in the end? Under glowing conifer from twin stars
hemmed not to be apart? You survived
        yourself, you survived in the ways in which lonely men desire to
in howling paleness. Crest of callus sickled where boots
    left earned scars, more skin than skin previously untested
            like plucked, naked heels of Mercury. The staff of sunlight guided
you through shoaling wildflowers made true by heartbreaths
        of jeweled insects. In messages from harped bodies,
        our species learned to embrace the possibility

            of music in the bluedark. Where you saw one person out, then
another
            a private epiphany was made more secret. Lungfuls
        of the Smoky Mountains where monked trees wore leaves like cassocks.
You went out against devotions that ask us to keep breathing—
        in scents of an old lover's shirt. Instead, you found

    a lush drive to live that appears in an old bull. You returned
with your backpack, the blued smell of animals
placed crookedly against my yellowed Manhattan walls. You returned with love
that would become so large. As if God gave you the chore to return
        with a missing calf. She lifted her head—
            to witness contrails making lazy crawls soften before disappearing.

The Teeth Lottery

Again, the television and this announcement:
any seven people bearing the same pattern of teeth
will win a grand prize larger than paradise. Smiling

like missionaries, searching for the saw
of a sharp and mean dogtooth and a crooked incisor,
mossy and curved like a river stone. Washing over

their desperation, some stopped closing their mouths
altogether, carrying metal tins and saliva tallying
their shirts. *Open wider. Like a shark. What do you have?*

Let me see. Under the moon, cold, unblinking eye,
widows yank their cavitied molars, one by one, daisy chain
each, and wear them like a grim medal. Then, their mouths

become vast, empty caves. No numbers tonight,
just a jumble of teeth of differing shapes and sizes,
yellow, cracked, or pearl white. And here I am, sinking

all my ungodly front teeth into the flesh of a crooked stone
fruit, juice running down. I eat olives and preserve
the middles jagged with meat. I never open voicemails.

I want to hear something new from a lover
in case we agree never to speak again. I hold onto
each part of myself. Unforgiven and perfect. I carry

a photograph of that lover taking a photograph of me
in the back pocket of my jeans. What is looting
versus preserving as a memento? I twist

my smile with lips sealed. I eat the center inward.

Nocturna

How slow is all of this dying? Across super county lines:
us, in the shine and fire of fossils. A small cat is in a steel trap.

A pale stray soul wandered into me,
and we drank good coffee. We couldn't undo dug latches
of what had come before. So, we made another day rot,

reorganizing what once was.
We know the beloved dead
    are the regrowth and yellow sere of stars.
How would they taste

in cannibalizing light? Disorder above, sightless.
    Planets mimic eyes.

    Where is the absent divine that doesn't cave or care?

    We,   too,   move on;   a catless girl cries for days   calling on a name

shared with songs   on the radio   that we   can only speculate.

On Lightness

And then during the blackout,
we gather storms from a lone cloud
loitering above

electric wires. Worried by sad calls
of night, mad ringing of things
dropped in the sink—

foraging for pale candles that light
up like spider's laced eggs once ignited.
How cruelly evolution rendered your heart

a flightless bird. Condemned to bite
each thorn off the crown, to order
like fossilized teeth. You fish out

a flashlight, clapped against the palm.
The sound awakens
the kitchen lights. Sleeping night,

taciturn birds. What if I could just
believe in love for its own sake.

In a delicate game of just listening
to the unseen genius of our lungs

between songs as if everything
was eternally reversible. Changing

the record over,
as if placing the sun
into another orange day.

The Contest

To win a free mattress, lovers sleep
apart, recognizing the other solely
through their partner's feral churning
of their mind that mirrors the awake
world soundtracked by their most private
music. The swell and ebb of their torsos, cheeks
tally-marked by pillows, the mantra of a contestant
murmuring a lost mother's name. I'm a mollusk
scouring my shell, halves of me sifting and seeking
subtleties through the white noise of sleep. A sculptor once said
every stone holds a form it yearns for—we, too, take shape
within our dreams. Where is that yearning
located? What have I carved myself into? A wick,
the orange innards twisted into flame. At the water's edge,
I've sprouted gills. When airborne, I mourn not being
the ocean. Listening to the nocturne of my lover's limbs,
the clear language of cicadas in the dark fields. His breath
was a ripple on a distant lake. I call his name. We claim our spoils.
Back home, on the newfound mattress, we lie on
the stone-cold floor. My graying hair spilling
all around his face. I've scrubbed the stains
of wines from the lips of lovers past. We leave
the door open in the shower. We eat sweet
clams from a tin, peeling through the concealed
bodies. I seek no prizes, no earthly inheritance.

The Flood and the Ark

1. ARK

We eat halved clementine on bedsheets. Circled like sun
in love's redeeming stains. A thirst that rolls each wave.
Lives spent devoted to comprehending an appetite.

On a cornflower-colored mattress, the world floats
on the fins of blue sharks. There, pulp and floods of nirvana,
of teeth and teeth. We are far and obscure in hidden water.

2. DOVE

Love nothing as brief as clouds. Only the sun makes love
as hot as the salt off the mule's rocky shoulders,
the mane braided with dandelions, each labor gently

bribed with sugar cubes to bite the bit. I dare you:
gift me your faith. Once, fingers tattooed with birdcages.
We are rings of doves. I know this glide is like a bow.

The Dive

The night is still ahead. Sing this knife
into the unrush of shellfish. Hush—
into smooth bodily knowing. Ungather

translucent skin. How sand is swept
from fisherman's cuticles.
Mussels curl on like floating ears. Listen

to the bright bristling nightbrush on
scour of hard rock. Brine bodies bowed
in oceanic prowl of half-moons.

Strum through stilled sealegs,
like a simple folk chord—creatures once
on an untouchable benthic floor.

The traps in the kitchen are humane.
Behind his eyelids in morning
light, humid perfume of open water.

He turns off the stove. Hands net
into a white dress, searching soft whips
of ocean line, catching my life in half-

heaven, between water and sky.
Tasting each—
other wet. So blissdrunk. So bluessalted.

Desire moving each
lazy applause of May rain.
Lips espying

another eternal hunger,
swimming toward
the coast, the moon is thinned to the fringe.

Haptics of Blue

With only the smallness of language
between us, the day before Krishna Janmashtami,
temple line, afternoon pressing in. The blond guru
marks our foreheads red. We are now right
holding a blood moon. In tender protest,
My world is another color. Lorca: *Verde que
te quiero verde.* Somewhere, a barn collapses,
flames fed on isolation. A runaway dog lapping a murky puddle
unaware of its master's devotion. You ask about separating
between cerulean and cornflower blue. My whole body is
asymmetrical. It might be part of inheritance of imbalance.
In Philadelphia, outside the Barnes Foundation,
in an iPhone's shadow: *Some love is silent labor,
windless and starless midnights.* I am yesterday's
relapse of repeated myths. What I don't know
is how to love another person. How will I remember
your wet, tangled hair smelled of kelp?
The horse-breath denim. Your shoulder's
gravity. We walk through, an exit sign
exhales. I tell you, *So, I want
to come clean.* In the parking lot, our private
ceremonies—a water bottle, your gentle face—
the red doesn't depart. My iPhone reminds me
to pray *salaat.* I am standing inside
our ancestor's afterlife. I don't know
what they hear.

Aubade in Another Universe

Caesura in a webbed supernova.
Spidered lightshivers
from the center. Atoms castled

in shooed seconds,
then—Universe. I am a self-taught
fluency. In the same weight and size,

a planetary
body crashes into
Earth. *Om* shivers in chrysalis.

Then, in false etymological offering:
ancient Sumerians believed in Nibiru,
a body as large as our own,

a planet that could obliterate us
on impact. On exactitude in science,
in false verses, *Nibiru* becomes *Habibi*.

That is what a Beloved is:
a collision. This is what love is:
an impact. *Oh, Habibi!*

Come, little planet.

A body that could meet us
in a drug of shared breath.
To hand ourselves into their air.

A body that is my physical antonym
and yet, each pink tantrum of kiss:
Oh, Nibiru! A body of the Beloved so

intoxicating, for every atom
belongs to me as good as it belongs to you.

Where should we crash?

Es otra mañana

I should have been
a pair of perfect scissors
choreographing through the fabric of time.

In chalks of interstellar messages
NASA sends *Across the Universe*
tumbling toward Polaris.

Pools of sorrow,
waves of joy. I'm bathing
in uncounted suds of deep space.

Above the liquor
cabinet: another sky. A drowsy
mouthful of wine is also an apology

to the Divine. How dare I stray
from this intoxication?
Fetal fist to mortal heart

flourishes to find the song of my childhood:
must, must, must. Nusrat Fateh Ali Khan
repeats *ecstasy, ecstasy, ecstasy,*

in channels of compulsory marrow. My *qawwali*—
a ruddy seismograph. In eight minutes
and twenty seconds, kiss me in the returned

skins of the sun. Pull
these sheets over our heads
and make it night. Each moon cloud

reminds—sweet signs
of my curled incisor
on the lateral of your tongue.

I want warmth the way oranges store
winter in their pulp. How far a dive—
into the ocean until each creature

becomes eyeless? I'm sieving through
each nautical mile for myself, glistening
like ancient sturgeons in the lakes

of America. Alive from the prehistoric,
so alien in earthly vulgarity.
Ancient Greeks wrestled rays

out of water dappled with the sun
to treat the body: wounds and tantrums
of the body. From the ocean,

we arrived. *Oh, Habibi.* We know
more about the sea than outer space.
There are more ways to imagine

than simply through signs. All language
is sign language, but this
is where our signs are

vital. One of our fingers is reserved
for orbiting in gold,
like a glamorous Saturn. One

of our fingers, a semaphore,
flickers our bodily rage.
Say this—with both hands: I want you

in this light-year. I want you, and that
is my most frugal prayer. I run
my hands all over, searching

for the hypsometry of your Rumi tattoo—
Oh, Habibi. Where the world's light entered you
with the odors of the moon. The bled ink

writing out verses. I open my mouth
forever to drink your skin, the color
the drops of Krishna. Tasting

the rebirth of my old tongue
in the way sunlight still leaks into
the windows of a burnt house,

of a red dawn over a pallid
stream of one night.
Trills of warble appear.

Fetal in their ring.
How old does this sound
go? Out of the sing of river—

I drink the divine, like horses
out of green buds about to speak
into spring. Won't you go on, *Habibi.*

The Earth returns. I'm following
you on a spiral. Another Universe
knows us. *Es otra mañana*

Where there are no borders.

I'll meet you there.
Us, again. In this event
horizon, *Habibi.*

Hold my hands
up palm to palm
so you may read them.

In an aubade in another
Universe, I am waiting for you
to annihilate me.

For annihilation
is the truest ecstasy.
for the Muslim saints

Es otra mañana

                              Salaam!   سلام

          سلام.

The Neighbors

The narcoleptic porch light swings envious of moths,
those nebulous sculptors of the bluest dark. Their surging

devotion to a false heat. They die for it, performing circles
as if my porch light is a holy structure. I am alone again

on a July night. The blue collie whimpers at my feet. She turns
over to show the scar on her belly. Thicker than the skin previous.

I translate in Urdu: *the stars gossip.* Constellations exchange hand
signs. All these lonely languages. Above, the moon performs

its usual inheritance, yowling light for creatures long
since departed. Arriving like a dead star's flash, a sudden physics

appears in the next-door driveway. There she is, my neighbor,
exhaling profanities for a lover. Every curse. She always leaves

her lights are on, and the lawn grows femur high. I see her
green toes and gummy slippers. She ashes the orange

dot of her cigarette and waves hello—
as if I'm an old friend. I hold up my hand and mouth

a muted *salaam.* سلام. Hello, stranger.

We have never spoken. It doesn't matter
if I make myself dinner now or keep on waving—

I will want something warm.

And I will wake up
wanting.

The Passenger

Neon gnawing dusk, plastic glow, a stranger
and I stop at a gas station. No miracle, just
the venison jerky reflecting the long teeth of city lights
and air fresheners, small forests
sealed in cellophane. Earlier, in the car,
out the windo*w*: *Deer!* Then, the dead one;
a body grotesque in its new shape. The swan
neck broken and eyes darkened with savage kindness.
There, from living to carcass. Metaphor's raw flesh
shaped into something unlike any animal.
I'm startled by beauty's lawlessness. The stranger
bites into the jerky. *Here,* he says, *you must be
so hungry.* In undergrad, a wealthy girl with perfect blood-
lacquered nails wrote about her hunter father, drunk,
an heir. Then, grad school, another girl,
Moby-Dick symbolism-armed, her father brought home
an albino deer. How they ate without reverence.
Just meat. Just dinner. What windows do I keep
looking through? What accumulates inside of me as I ride
here now, this mining town's gas station where
there are wooden souvenirs, a moose, a two-headed calf,
and cheap nameplates that never fit my name.
Above, a sculpture rotates.
Turning on string: a rotation of coal and a lightbulb
tethered by driftwood. Gravity holds,
heavy in multiple configurations. There is a portrait
of the artist: a coal miner, lungs turned to stone. Imagine
his nailbeds. His tender bread. The contours of his
young widowed wife. I understand. The motel after,
I leave the lights off. The stranger wordlessly
dissolves to his room. I recite a prayer, whatever I have
memorized, and sleep on a worn sheet
of perfect darkness. Waiting. I will drape it over
the next deer.

Acknowledgments

First, to the reader: thank you.

I offer my thanks to my family—my beloveds—and to the vast, unknowable shape that surrounds us. Thanks Mama Jaan, Papa, and Meira. For it all.

I am incredibly thankful for all my writing professors and mentors at the University of Utah and Columbia University: Aracelis Girmay, Major Jackson, Jay Deshpande, Cynthia Cruz, Timothy Donnelly, Deborah Paredez, Alan Gilbert, Shane McCrae, Monica Youn, Katharine Coles, Paisley Rekdal, Stephen Goldsmith, especially Dr. Brett Clark—a special thanks to you. And thank you to Lucie Brock-Broido's spectral presence.

I would like to express my gratitude to my Columbia University peers: Mark Gregory Lopez, Shyanne Figueroa Bennett, Elias Sorich, Timothy Emile Lax, Antonio Addessi, Emma Ginader, Peter Patapis, Robiny Jamerson, and Rachel Kang. Thank you for being here first.

Thank you to Smith College and Leila Chatti for giving *Desire/Halves,* a fraction of these poems, its first life and orbit Thank you, Adrie. Thank you, Sylvia. You remain, always.

Thank you to The Ohio State University Press, Marcus Jackson, and all staff of *The Journal.*

To the editors who gave these poems a place in their silence or their choosing, thank you. Thank you to everyone who pulled my words from the slush pile. Thank you, slush.

To my fellow artists, friends, and muses: Cameron J. Jorgensen, Dane J. Horton, Patrick J. Bayly, Basie Allen, Aaron H. Aceves, Jack Scott Holmes, Brian Chander Wiora, Todd Goddard, Nat Blanton, Grayson del Faro, Caleb Milne, Jeff Sorensen, Jonah King, Corley Miller, Daniel Leipow, Jordan Nemelka, Zakary Sonntag, Amber Aumiller, Rylee Syme, Erica O'Brien, Blaise Swing, Gabrielle Bates, and Maxwell Ijams.

Recently, Cam shared an anecdote from his time working door-to-door. An elderly man said to him, "How do you know if you're the one who originated a thought about someone, or if that person was already thinking of you? So, you thought of them?" Well, I am thinking of you. I promise.

I love you, Natalia C. Abril. You asked for poems. I wrote them. I love you and thank you for your unwavering encouragement and introduction to devotion.

And finally, there is no one I must thank more than my husband, Dr. John C. Dulin—my freckled best friend. Many of these poems were written before I knew you; in your absence, they asked their questions. For eternity, Blue.

To borrow from Rilke: All of it, perhaps, was a preparation—to find you again.

To God, whose presence remains sovereign and concealed, yet constant in my life.

Thank God for every poet.

I have love for each.

Some poems in this collection appeared earlier in the following venues:
    "Stringing the Bow," *Virginia Quarterly Review*
    "Maggotville," *The Boiler*
    "Marrow of Mercy," *Australian Poetry Journal*
    "Good Girl," *ONLY POEMS* (finalist for the Leonard Cohen Poetry Prize)
    "The Strangers," *Amsterdam Review*
    "The Waiters," *The American Poetry Review*
    "The Brute," *Narrative Magazine*
    "On Hunger," *Southern Humanities Review*
    "On Greek Origins," *Cream City Review*
    "Self Portrait of a Face That Isn't Mine," *Virginia Quarterly Review*
    "The Cavesleepers," *Virginia Quarterly Review*
    "The Divine Dyslexia," *RHINO Poetry* (2025 Ralph Hamilton Editors' Prize)
    "The Zikr Room," *Mizna: Journal*
    "Girlish," *The Scores*
    "In the Throats of Wild Things," *Image Journal*
    "Lucky Rabbit's Foot," *The Journal*
    "In Dead Horse Point, We Are Alone," *The American Poetry Review*
    "The Eyeball Halves," *Southeast Review* (first section, as "Arrival, in Halves")
    "Aleph from What Was Once a Homeland," *Denver Quarterly*
    "One Red Thread," *Borderlands: Texas Poetry Review*
    "Brief Conversations with a Little Moon," *Anthropocene*
    "How to Make an Ariel," *The Margins*
    "Brine," *Notre Dame Review*
    "Toward Tenderness, a Knife," *SLUG Magazine*
    "And the Word for Moonlight Is My Name," *Poetry Magazine*
    "Con la Serpiente II," *Small Orange Journal*
    "Still, Life with Fruit," *Brushfire Magazine*
    "Pegasus Tattoo on the Left," *Four Way Review* (later republished on *Poetry Daily*)
    "Vultures, Then," *The Rumpus*
    "The Last of Us in the Wild," *Wildness*
    "The Mouths," *The Boiler*
    "The Appalachian Trail," *Black Warrior Review*
    "The Teeth Lottery," *Cream City Review*

"Nocturna," *The American Poetry Review*
"On Lightness," *Foothill Poetry Journal*
"The Contest," *Virginia Quarterly Review*
"The Flood and the Ark," *Raleigh Review* (as "The Flood" and "The Ark")
"The Dive," *Black Warrior Review*
"Haptics of Blue," *Image Journal*
"The Neighbors," *The Arkansas International*
"The Passenger," *The Oxonian Review*

In addition, some poems appeared in earlier form in my chapbook, *Desire/Halves* published by Nine Syllables Press.

The *Journal* Charles B. Wheeler Poetry Prize